BOSWORTH EDITION.

No 82.

Anton Rubinstein said:-
"The more I play the more thoroughly I am convinced
that the Pedal is the soul of the Piano; there are
cases where the Pedal is everything."

Guide

to the proper use of the

Pianoforte Pedals

with examples
out of the Historical Concerts
of

ANTON RUBINSTEIN.

translated from the German
by
John A. Preston.
This work is also published in French and German

— ∙ —

BOSWORTH & C°.
WIEN I.
LEIPZIG.   PARIS.
LONDON W.   ZÜRICH.
New-York, T. B. Harms & Francis Day & Hunter.

Printed in the United States .

Anton Rubinstein:

Guide to the Proper use of the Pianoforte Pedals.

Facsimile of 1897 edition.

First published Bosworth & Co. 1897.

Republished Travis & Emery 2009.

Published by
Travis & Emery Music Bookshop
17 Cecil Court, London, WC2N 4EZ, United Kingdom.
(+44) 20 7240 2129
neworders@travis-and-emery.com

Hardback: ISBN10: 1-904331-93-9   ISBN13: 978-1904331-93-3
Paperback: ISBN10: 1-904331-94-7   ISBN13: 978-1-904331-94-0

Anton Grigorevich Rubinstein (1829-1894), Russian pianist, composer and conductor.
Elder brother of Nikolai.
(Not related to Arthur).

More details available from
- Stanley Sadie: The New Grove Dictionary of Music and Musicians.
- http://en.wikipedia.org/wiki/Anton_Rubinstein

Further reading, in English:
- Anton Rubinstein: Autobiography, 1829-1889. 1890.
- A. Hervey: Rubinstein. London, 1913.
- Alexander McArthur : Anton Rubinstein, A Biographical Sketch. Adam & Charles Black, Edinburgh, 1889.
- Catherine Bowen: Free Artist: The Story of Anton and Nicholas Rubinstein. Little Brown, 1939.
-Larry Sitsky: Anton Rubinstein: An Annotated Catalog of Piano Works and Biography. Greenwood Press, 1998
- Philip S. Taylor: Anton Rubinstein: A Life in Music. Indiana University Press, 2007

BOSWORTH EDITION.

Nº 82

Guide

to the proper use of the

Pianoforte Pedals

with examples
from the Historical Concerts
of

ANTON RUBINSTEIN.

BOSWORTH EDITION.

N° 82.

Anton Rubinstein said:-
"The more I play the more thoroughly I am convinced
that the Pedal is the soul of the Piano; there are
cases where the Pedal is everything."

Guide
to the proper use of the

Pianoforte Pedals

with examples
out of the Historical Concerts
of

Anton Rubinstein.

translated from the German
by
John A. Preston.
This work is also published in French and German

——————

BOSWORTH & C°.

LEIPZIG.   WIEN I.   PARIS.
LONDON W.   ZÜRICH.

New-York, T. B. Harms & Francis Day & Hunter.

Printed in the United States.

Contents.

Preface.

The question of the importance and use of the pedal has been very insufficiently treated in pianoforte literature; neither in the newer, nor in the older methods for this instrument has attention been directed to the fundamental rules governing its use.

Hummel, for example, does not mention the pedal once as absolutely necessary, no matter what the passage. The use of the pedal as a means of tone-painting was evidently quite unknown to him, one of the greatest virtuosos of his time. Czerny, in his chapter regarding its use, gives no definite rules, saying merely that it is to be used where it is indicated by the composer, and not used in places where such indication fails. The composers themselves often make no mention of the pedal, or indicate its employment in a false or indefinite manner. Schumann, for instance, often makes use of the indefinite phrase " Mit Ped.," which leaves entirely vague the question where the pedal is to be used, and where released. Beethoven indicates its use also by means of a general phrase " Senza Sordini," = without dampers, = with raised dampers, = with pedal. The greater number of modern pianists govern themselves more by their own personal taste than by any definite principles.

A proper and careful use of the pedal is, however, of great importance in pianoforte playing. The most general rules of interpretation cannot, in many cases, be accurately carried out without its use. Beyond this the pedal adds power, euphony and fulness to the tone, and appears, thanks to these qualities, as a most useful assistant in good phrasing and shading. Lastly the pedal often produces alone those effects which, in the interpretation of some great artist, awaken our most profound astonishment.

The false use of the pedal, on the contrary, hinders often the proper definition of a musical phrase, disturbs the clearness of the melody and harmony, causes even at times a direct deformation of the latter, and induces in general faults of every description. For this reason it is necessary to define clearly the principles of its use, by which the great artists, if even at times unconsciously, govern themselves.*

The historical concerts of Anton Rubinstein bear very directly upon this question. They are important as showing the use made of the pedal by a great artist in works published during the past three centuries.

The greater part of the observations and conclusions contained in this guide have been drawn from this source, to which, in a few instances, the employment made of the pedal by Nicholas Rubinstein has been added. The examples here given are taken almost entirely from compositions played by Anton Rubinstein in his historical concerts.

Exceptions thereto are Examples 21, 58—60, 93, 97, and those given in Paragraph 6 of the Introductory Remarks.

---

* An explanation of such principles is found only in two works, i. e., those of H. Schmitt and L. Köhler.

Introductory Remarks.

1. Manner of using the Pedal.

The use of the pedal demands two movements:

a. The downward pressure (down pedal).

b. The upward release (up pedal).

The pedal is always pressed down to its fullest extent.   (Figure 1 .)

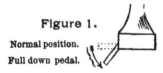

Figure 1.

Normal position.
Full down pedal.

The release of the pedal follows in two ways:

1. Either the pedal is allowed to resume its former horizontal position (full release, Figure 2):

2. Or released enough to resume an intermediate position (half release, Figure 3).

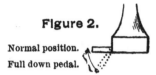

Figure 2.

Normal position.
Full down pedal.

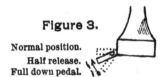

Figure 3.

Normal position.
Half release.
Full down pedal.

When the pedal is used to its fullest extent in both directions, such use is called full pedal; when, after a full downward pressure, it is allowed to return only to an intermediate position, such use is called half pedal; when the half pedal is used repeatedly and as rapidly as possible, so that the foot seems almost to vibrate, such use is called tremolo half pedal.

2. Pedal Marks.

The pedal is usually indicated as follows: the down pedal by this abbreviation *Ped.*; the release (up pedal) by this sign ✻.   (Example 1a.)

In this guide other marks which are more definite and easily understood will be used for this purpose, viz.: the sign ⌊ for down, and the sign ⌋ for up pedal will be placed under the notes respectively affected. (Example 1 b.)

B.&Co.2193.

If the up pedal follows soon after the down, the sign ⌐ will be employed. (Example 2.)

A very short down pedal, followed immediately by its release, will be indicated by means of upright lines (||). (Example 3.)

The use of the down pedal *after* the note to be influenced has been struck (called in future the secondary pedal) is indicated by a horizontal dash through the upright line ⊥———. (Example 4, see also page 7.)

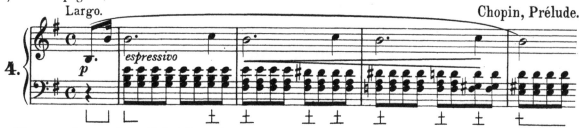

The secondary pedal which follows immediately upon the up pedal is indicated by this sign ⊥
(Example 4.)

The half pedal is indicated in three following ways:

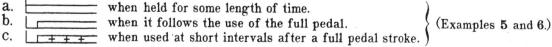

a. ⊏———— when held for some length of time.
b. ⌐———— when it follows the use of the full pedal.
c. ⌐—+—+—+— when used at short intervals after a full pedal stroke.

(Examples 5 and 6.)

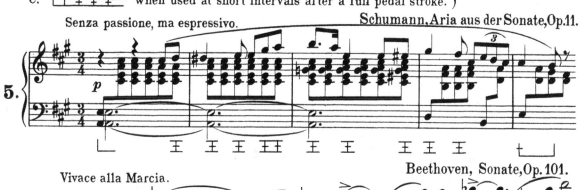

The tremolo half pedal is indicated by the sign ⌞ .... (Example 7.)

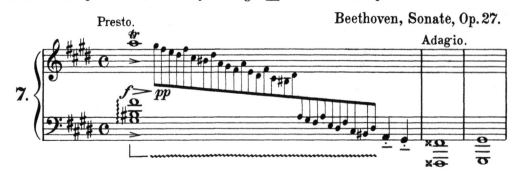

3. Effect of the Full and Half Pedal upon the Dampers.

When a key is struck the damper is thereby raised, allowing the tone to continue vibrating; when the key is released the damper drops upon the wire, and shuts off the tone. The pedal raises all the dampers simultaneously, whereby the tone still continues, even after the fingers have left the keys. The full use of the pedal makes possible a continued tone throughout all that part of the keyboard which is influenced by dampers. The full release of the pedal shuts off suddenly the vibration of all tones influenced by dampers. The half pedal influences differently the upper and lower parts of the pianoforte; the change from full to half pedal shuts off the upper and middle tones, but has only slight effect upon the lower ones.

4. Phonetic Pauses.

The pedal causes the tone to vibrate after the finger has left the key, as has been already stated, thereby taking the place of the latter, and setting it free. (Examples 8–10.)

Moderato maestoso.   Cui, Polonaise.

10.

Such pauses are designated phonetic or vibrating pauses. These latter are met with very frequently in modern pianoforte playing, and form a characteristic distinction between the old and new schools of piano literature, the former not knowing the necessity for the use of such pauses.

5. The Primary and Secondary Pedal and Half Pedal.

When the pedal or half pedal is employed simultaneously with the stroke upon the key, this use is called the primary pedal. (Example 1, page 4.) When, upon the other hand, it is pressed down immediately after the note is struck, such use is called the secondary pedal. (Examples 4-6, page 5.) This latter is most widely employed. Good pianoforte players make much greater use of it than of the primary pedal.

6. The Acoustic Properties of the Pianoforte.

Every musical tone, which seems to us only a single tone of a certain pitch, possesses in fact the following secondary or sympathetic tones :

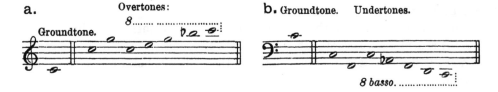

The first set are called overtones, the second undertones. All these tones are so weak that they can hardly be distinguished by the ordinary ear. Their existence, however, may be easily proved by striking the little c strongly and staccato after carefully depressing the great C. In this case the tone of the little c will vibrate so long as the great C is held down. The above is made clear by the following example :

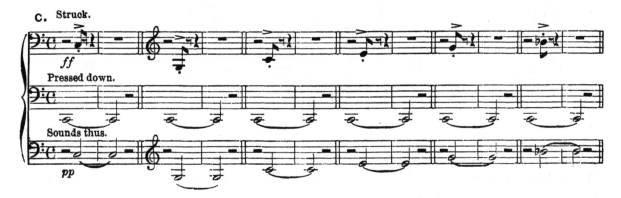

In the same manner the existence of the remaining overtones may also be proved, as shown in the following example ·

The secondary tones may also be heard, even though not as distinctly, if the one tone is pressed down at the instant the other is struck. The existence of these secondary tones may also be shown by pressing down carefully at first the secondary key, and then striking the principal note. The act of pressing down the key raises its damper, and thereby makes it possible for the strings of this secondary tone to vibrate. A similar pressure upon any keys standing in such relation to a given principal note causes a more or less distinct tone; such pressure upon other notes, upon the contrary, has no effect.

The down pedal employed at the moment of striking a note raises all the dampers simultaneously, freeing in this manner all the strings, and allowing all secondary tones, in proportion to their relation with the principal note, to vibrate. This fact explains the difference between the full and rich tone of a note played with the pedal and that of one without.

The presence of undertones may be shown in a similar, simple manner. Holding the pedal, strike the one-lined c (c̲) sharply and staccato, then press down carefully the little c, and raise the pedal. The one-lined c (c̲) will continue to sound as long as the little c is held. This is explained by the following diagram.

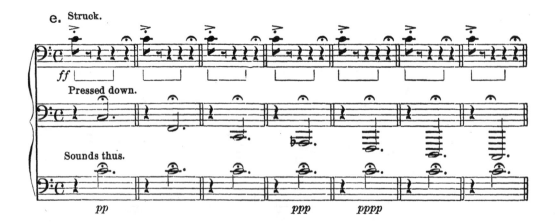

The existence of the remaining undertones may be shown in the same way. These latter are, however, weaker than the overtones.

The above will be found a sufficient explanation of the physical data, as well as of the purely pedal effects mentioned at the end of the first chapter (Function 16), and also of the general rules governing the use of the pedal, which are mentioned in this Guide.

Chapter I.

The Functions of the Pedal.

Function 1. The pedal makes possible the continued vibration of a tone after the finger has left the key. (Examples 11 and 12.)

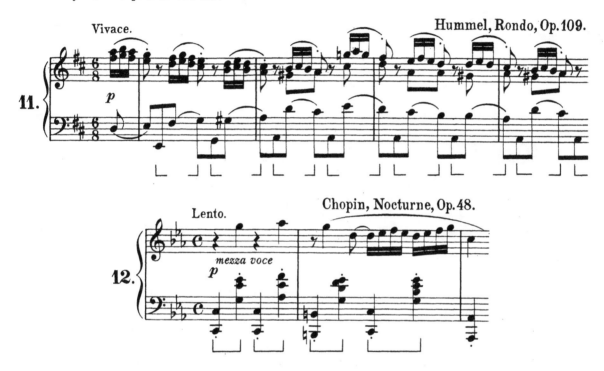

Function 2. The pedal makes it possible for tones to vibrate together which cannot be struck simultaneously by the fingers. In this connection it is employed for the following purposes:

a. To bind together tones which lie more than an octave apart. (Example 13.)

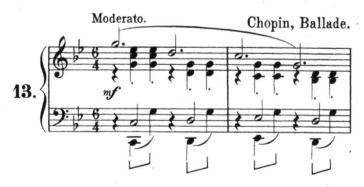

In this case the pedal causes the first tone to continue vibrating after the finger has left the key, being raised at the moment when the second note is struck. If more than two notes are to be bound together by its use, the pedal must be raised as each new note is struck, and at once thereafter again pressed down, *i. e.* the so-called secondary pedal (Chapter III) must be used. This use of the pedal is here necessary, in order that the hands and pedal shall not be raised at the same instant, which would be the case in its primary use, and as a consequence of which the legato character of the passage would be lost.

b. To bind together such notes of a melody as are played with the same finger, or with fingers whereby a legato connection is either exeedingly difficult or impossible. (Examples 14 and 15.)

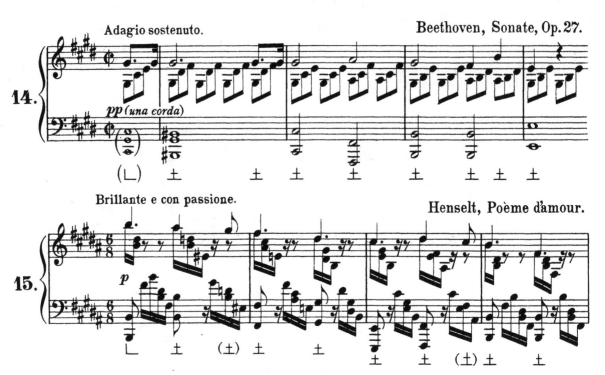

c. To bind together double notes and chords where a legato could only otherwise be attained by means of a glissando, or by the substitution of other fingers or of the thumb. These two means are not alone sufficient, for a glissando produces no clear tone, and such a substitution as above indicated is only possible during a moderate tempo, and not always even then. Here, also, the secondary pedal appears as a most simple and effective means of binding together the chords, while the so-called phonetic pauses fill in the breaks made necessary by the stroke. (Examples 16–20.)

Function 3. The pedal makes it possible for the tones of one voice to continue vibrating while the fingers are used to play the notes of another voice which lies more than an octave removed from the first. (Example 21.)

In modern compositions there occur many double notes and extended chords which cannot be played even by persons possessing a large hand, in spite of the fact that the separate tones are intended to vibrate simultaneously. In such cases the double notes or chords must be played arpeggiando with the pedal, pressing down the latter with the first note. The quicker the arpeggio is executed in this case, the nearer it will approach the interpretation intended by the composer. The secondary pedal is naturally not to be used in such cases. (Examples 22–24.)

12

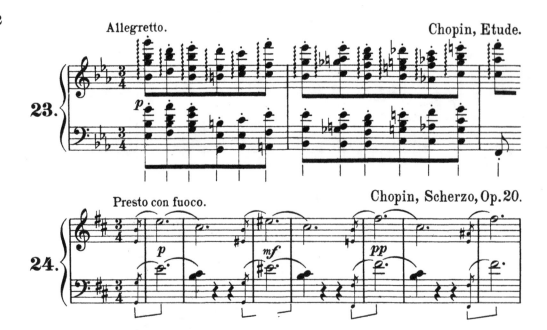

Function 4. The pedal makes the further vibration of a principal voice possible when the fingers are needed for a secondary part, either in form of an harmonic or other figure, or of a chord. (Examples 8–10, pages 6 and 7.)

In such cases the pedal makes possible the execution, with one hand, of passages which would otherwise, in some instances, be impossible with two hands, or even more.

Remark. Thanks to this pedal function, two-hand transcriptions are made possible which compete with orches, tral scores in fulness: transcriptions of Thalberg, Liszt, Tausig, Henselt, etc. In this category belong also the transcriptions of Anton Rubinstein, unfortunately not published, which he played in his series of historical concerts- Beethoven's Egmont Overture, and Mendelssohn's Wedding March.

When the accompaniment to a phonetic pause is elaborated by means of arpeggios or other harmonic figures, the first note thereof is generally the long note of the melody, which is held in vibration by the pedal. Such pauses are not only ornamented by means of purely harmonic figures, but also by various miscellaneous passages, including sometimes even scales.

The pedal is employed also to effect the continued vibration of double notes and chords which form the theme, through which means the hand, thereby made free, can carry out the bass accompaniment during these pauses by means of downward jumps, or in other cases can execute high notes by jumping upward. By means of the secondary pedal double notes and chords may not only be held their full length of time, but also be connected in a legato manner. (Example 25.)

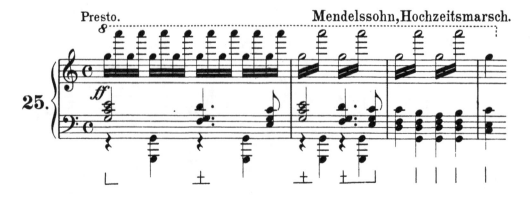

Chords forming an accompaniment, and executed during such phonetic pauses by the hands made free by the use of the pedal may also be varied, if an accented chord in a low position is kept in vibration at the same time by means of the pedal. (Example 26.)

Function 5. The pedal is also employed when shorter chords, serving as an accompaniment, are played during the life of, and in the same part of the instrument as, the melodic note. In such cases the long note of the melody is struck forcibly, and carried on by the pedal, while the same or the other hand plays lightly the notes forming the accompaniment. (Example 27.)

To this function belongs the case of two voices which enter one after the other, playing the same notes, under circumstances which render difficult the exact execution of the passage. (Example 28.)

B. & Co. 2193.

Function 6. The pedal is used to give additional tone to a note in legato playing, when the power of the finger alone is insufficient.

Such use of the pedal makes possible the production of very loud tones, either by use of the wrist movement, or by using the weight of the whole hand. The pedal here serves to retain the legato indicated by the composer which would be otherwise interrupted for the purpose of attaining the requisite amount of tone.

In this case, also, the secondary pedal is employed. (Example 29.)

Function 7. The pedal is used for the purpose of giving special stress to one note of a chord; in such instances the hand is freed to attain the proper position for the stroke.

It is understood that the finger selected for this purpose must be pushed slightly forward and held firmly, a trifle beyond the others. This is most easily brought about if the hand is free of the notes. The use of the pedal makes the hand free to strike such a note by means of the wrist or arm movement, while the requisite position is attained during the phonetic pause. Should a legato execution of these double notes or chords be demanded, it may be obtained by the use of the secondary pedal. (Example 30.)

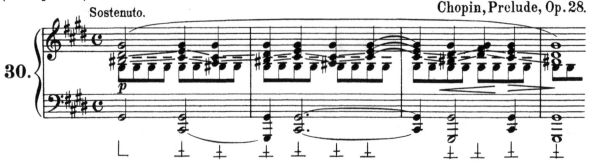

Function 8. The pedal is employed to give a short rest to the hand after or during the execution of a long and extended chord passage; by this means the hand is raised from the notes and momentarily released of tension. This use of the pedal makes it possible to execute to the end without especial fatigue the many instances of this nature which occur in modern pianoforte literature. The Chopin Polonaise in A flat, Op. 53, is a good example of this use of the pedal.

Remark. Even Anton Rubinstein, who possessed such well-known endurance, often made use of the above.

Function 9. The vibration of a long extended tone is made even longer by the use of the pedal in cases where tones nearly related to it are struck repeatedly during its continuance. (Example 31.)

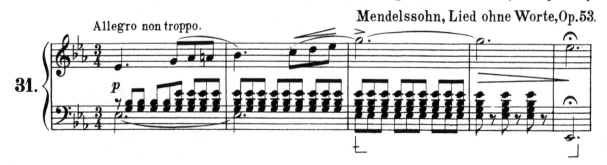

The four following functions (10-13) relate to the use of the pedal in phrases and nuances.

Function 10. The pedal is used at the beginning of a musical phrase or a rhythmical figure, but not at the end. (Examples 32-35.)

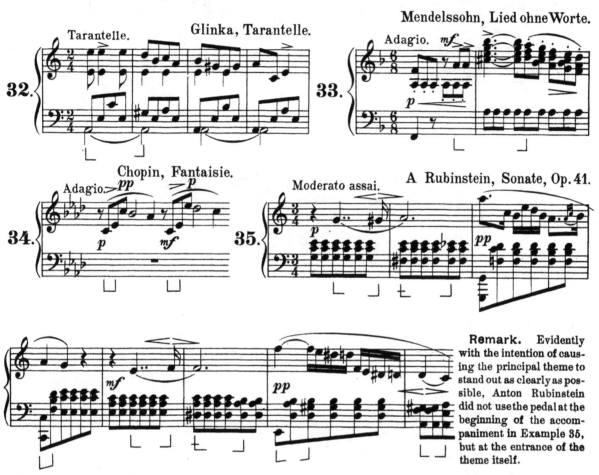

Remark. Evidently with the intention of causing the principal theme to stand out as clearly as possible, Anton Rubinstein did not use the pedal at the beginning of the accompaniment in Example 35, but at the entrance of the theme itself.

Function 11. The pedal is used during a crescendo passage, especially in one having an ascending melody, carrying, in such cases, neither crescendo nor pedal quite to the highest note of the melody. The diminuendo following is played without pedal. (Examples 36-40.)

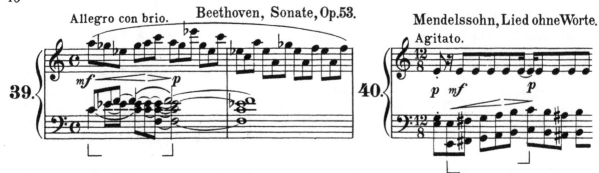

The pedal is also sometimes used in a descending crescendo melody or passage. (Example 41.)

Function 12. When the same phrase is repeated in various degrees of tone, the stronger is played with, and the lighter without the pedal, or at least with a very moderate use thereof. (Examples **42–45**.)

Chopin, Valse, Op. 34

Vivace.

44.

Chopin, Prélude.

Sostenuto.

45.

Function **13.** The pedal increases and sharpens the contrast between two phrases of different character. (Examples **46-48.**)

Allegro maestoso.

Chopin, Polonaise, Op. 40. Nº 2.

46.

Tschaikowsky, Valse-Scherzo, Op. 7.

47.

Mesto.

Chopin, Mazurka, Op. 33. Nº 4.

48.

Function 14. The pedal may give a purely orchestral coloring to a pianoforte: when alternating groups of notes like the following occur, the pedal should be used in the one phrase, and omitted in the other. (Examples 49-53.)

20

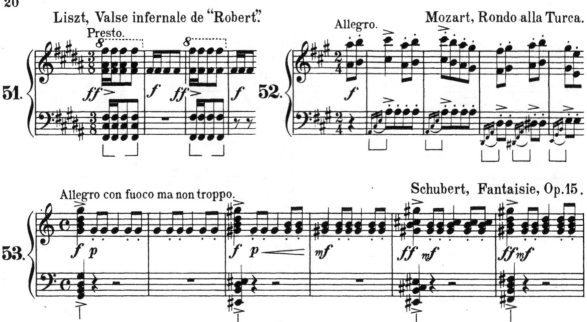

Remark. It is by such uses of the pedal, combined with great variety of touch, that one is able to explain partially the great diversity of tone color which characterized Anton Rubinstein's playing.

In the following paragraphs the pedal appears as a necessary help in the execution of purely artistic problems.

Function 15. The pedal gives an indefinite, undefined, and cloudy character to a passage, making possible the approximate imitation of rustling and rushing of the wind, thunder, gusts of wind, etc. (Examples 54–57.)

In the Finale of the Chopin Sonata (Example 54) Rubinstein intended to imitate gusts of wind by a brief use of the pedal upon the descending scale.

In the Chopin Cradle Song (Example 55) the constant use of the pedal in each measure, and the *pp*, which characterizes the entire course of the piece, were intended to convey the idea of dream pictures suggesting themselves to a child, who is gradually lulled to sleep by the regular motion of the cradle.

In the Schumann Fantaisie (Example 56) the pedal is employed with similar artistic intentions. In this case the marking is that used by Nicholas Rubinstein. To this paragraph belongs also the Chopin Funeral March (from the same Sonata) as played by Anton Rubinstein. In order to represent the approach of the procession, he used the secondary pedal at first for every quarter (♩) bar (*pp* and *p*), then for every half (♩) bar, (*f*), and at last for the whole bar, (*ff*), employing the same means in reverse order to represent the gradual disappearance of the procession.

In example 57 Anton Rubinstein employed the pedal at half measure intervals in order to represent the absolute, passionless rest which prevails in this aria, and which finds expression in the words, "The reconciliation of a soul, passing to a better world, with all earthly sorrow."

Function 16. This last function shows the pedal employed to cause the vibration of secondary tones, * as also the tones of preceding chords or passages. (Examples 58–60.)

Beethoven, Sonate, Op. 27.

*) *The effect above indicated will be easily attained if the pedal is released, in the following examples, after carefully pressing down the keys of the corresponding relative or sympathetic tones.*

B.&Co. 2193

Chapter II.

The Primary Pedal.

The primary pedal is used:

1. At the beginning of a piece.

2. After a pause common to both hands, and also after such breaks in the course of a piece as are not designated as pauses, and yet are necessary to its proper execution.

In these cases the secondary pedal may take the place of the primary if the peculiar effect of increase of tone (see Chapter III, 2) is intended to be produced.

In the two following examples, however, such exchange is quite impossible.

3. In passages of staccato notes and chords, for the purpose of giving extra fulness and power.

Chopin, Ballade, Op. 52.

Naturally in this case the pedal must not be held longer than the individual notes themselves.

4. In quick broken chords and jumps, which have a greater compass than one octave, and generally in quick arpeggios.   (Examples 22–24.)

Chapter III.

The Secondary Pedal.

The secondary pedal is employed in a wide variety of ways in modern pianoforte playing, and much oftener than the primary.

1. The secondary pedal is used principally to avoid the lack of clearness which would arise in legato playing if the foot were pressed down at the exact moment of striking the key.   Such lack of clearness arises from the following mechanical fact: the finger leaves the key in a legato passage, either at the moment when the next note is struck, or occasionally, and for the sake of even greater tone connection, a trifle later ; and as the dampers which stop the vibration follow exactly the above motions of the fingers, it will readily be seen that in the first case, and even more in the second, the damper will hardly have dropped upon the wire when it will be again raised by the re-entrance of the pedal exactly with the next note.   As a result of this, two notes are heard, the new one and the former, which the pedal has, so to say, caught up.   The secondary pedal does away entirely with such unclearness of tone.   (Examples 62 and 63.)

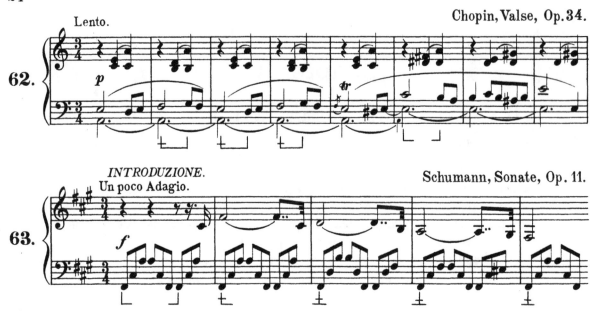

Lento.

Chopin, Valse, Op. 34.

62.

INTRODUZIONE.
Un poco Adagio.

Schumann, Sonate, Op. 11.

63.

2. The secondary pedal has further the property of causing a peculiar tone color, from the fact that by its use the tone is slightly strengthened while being held. (Example 64.)

Chopin, Etude, Op. 25.

Lento.

64.

pp smorzando.

ppp

Chapter IV.
Changing or Raising the Pedal.

The pedal is changed or raised :

1. At a change of harmony.

Remark. Exceptions to this rule are passages where such harmonic change occurs in the upper part of the piano-forte (Example 65), or where the pedal is used to increase the power of a crescendo, to imitate thunder, noise, etc. (Chapter I, Function 15.)

Allegro.

Schubert-Liszt, Valse (Soirée de Vienne.)

65.

pp

mf

2. At the entrance of a new melodic note, especially one foreign to the harmony. (Examples 66 and 67.)

Chapter V.

The Most Important Conditions for the Non-Use of the Pedal.

The pedal must not be used:

1. In a regular succession of notes (especially ascending) in the middle and lower portion of the pianoforte, without harmonic accompaniment, in moderate or slow tempo, and where the separate notes have a similar amount of tone. (Examples 68 and 69.)

In the upper portion of the instrument (which is not supplied with dampers) the pedal may be used under such circumstances.

Remark. The pedal can be used only very sparingly in older polyphonic works, and then only for a short time, because these works are played principally in a moderate tempo, are written for the middle portion of the pianoforte, and contain comparatively few harmonic figures.

B.&Co. 2193

2. The pedal cannot even well be used in harmonic figures if the voices therein lie near to each other, and in the lower part of the pianoforte; the use of the pedal with the major chord in such cases is to be avoided. As an exception to this rule may be mentioned cases where the effect of a rustle or noise is intended, in which cases the pedal may be used at will. (See Chapter I, Function 15.)

3. The pedal must not be used in a decrescendo passage in quick tempo, especially when going from *ff* to *pp*.

Remark. Nicholas Rubinstein used the pedal even under above conditions, changing it constantly in order to avoid any unclearness of tone: at the end of the decrescendo he used the second (left) pedal also. (Example 70.)

A pianist who is not thoroughly a master of the pedal should preferably avoid its use in such cases.

4. When a strong diminuendo is demanded at the end of a phrase or rhythmic figure, the pedal should not be employed with the last notes. (See Chapter I, Function 10, and Examples 32–35.

5. The pedal should furthermore not be used in the repetition (*pp*) of a phrase which has previously been played strongly and with the pedal. (Chapter I, Function 12, and Examples 42–45.

6. Similarly the pedal must not be used in a descending figure with strong diminuendo, when this is to be followed by an ascending figure with strong crescendo and pedal. (Chapter I, Function 11, and Examples 36–40.)

7. In a phrase which is to be played staccato, or very lightly and elastically, the pedal is not to be used, especially when such phrase follows directly upon one of an opposite character where it has been employed. (Examples 71–73 ; see also Chapter I, Function 13, and Examples 46–48.)

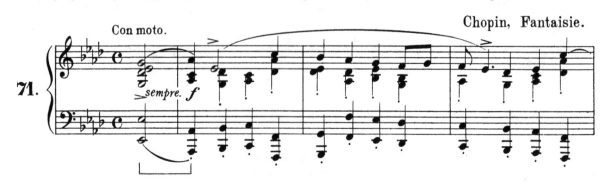

Vivace capriccioso.   Glinka, Souvenir d'une Mazurka.

72.

Tschaikowsky, Valse-scherzo, Op. 7.

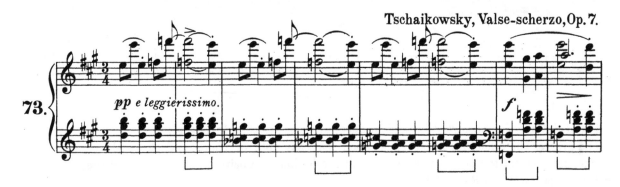

73.

8. The pedal must also not be used in *pp* passages where great distinctness and clearness are demanded.

As examples may be mentioned "Bird as Prophet" and "Traumeswirren" of Schumann, "Au Bord d'un Source" by Liszt, and the Finale of the B-flat minor Sonata of Chopin.

Remark. Anton Rubinstein used in these cases the left, but never at the same time the right pedal, excepting where a special increase of tone is demanded, when he made use of the latter. (See Example 54, and the *f* and *ff* passages in the "Traumeswirren" of Schumann, etc.

9. Finally the pedal must not be used in passages where no great fulness of tone is desired in the accompaniment. (Example 74.)

Mozart, Fantaisie, Op. 11.

74.

Chapter VI.

Use of the Pedal in Scale Passages and Harmonic Figures.

§1. Use of the Pedal in Scale Passages.

Scales, and passages formed from them, are executed with the pedal under the following conditions:

1. When a bass note or chord is played f either immediately preceding or simultaneously with a scale passage of light or crescendo character. (Example 75.)

The pedal may be more readily used in descending scales than in ascending.

The greater the difference in power between the bass note or chord and the scale passage, the quicker and lighter the latter is executed, and the higher its position upon the pianoforte, the more justifiable is the use of the pedal.

The pedal may be employed with even greater freedom provided such note or chord is repeated while the scale passage is executed, or if the scale passage is accompanied by an harmonic figure in quick motion. (Examples 76–80.)

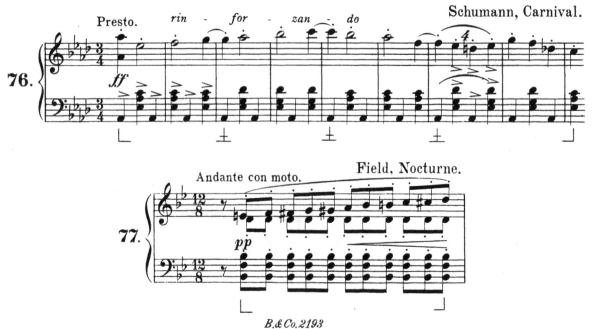

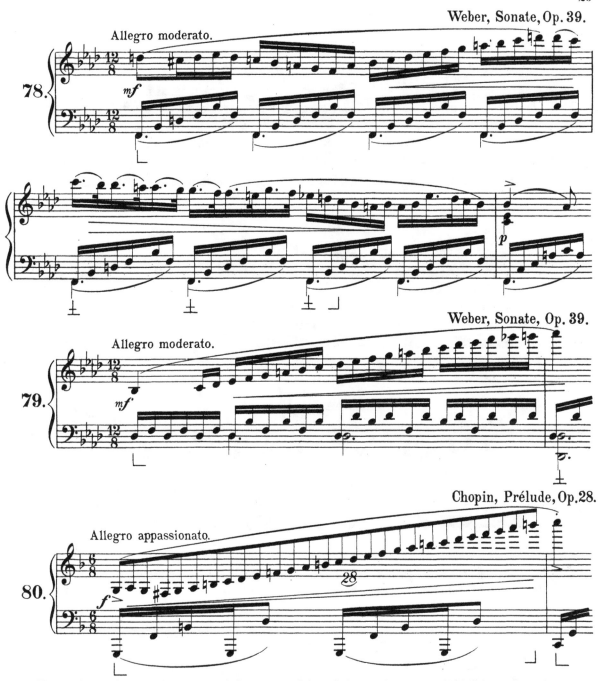

Under these circumstances, a scale passage with pedal sounds very well if it begins **pp**, in a high position, and is followed by a downward crescendo. (Example 81.)

The more prominent the accompaniment in such cases, the more possible is the use of the pedal. (Example 82).

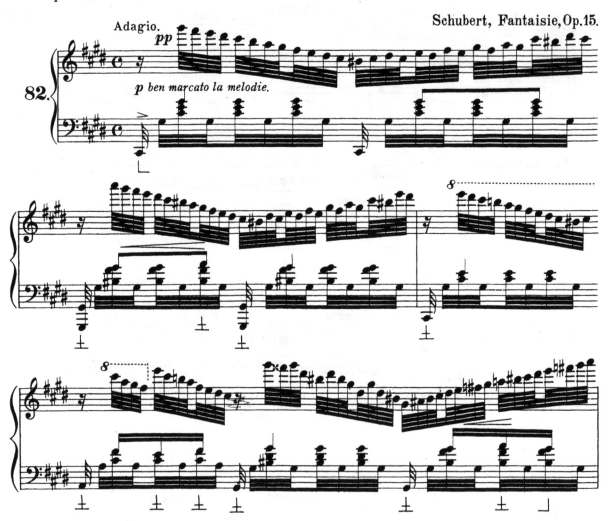

2. The pedal may usually be employed also in cases where the sustained or repeated chords, notes or harmonic figures lie higher than the scale passage. (Example 83.)

3. The pedal is often used as well in scale passages without accompaniment, in cases where the composer wishes to give the impression of noise, thunder, etc. (Chapter I, Functions 11 and 15.)

4. Chromatic scale passages may also be similarly treated with the pedal, more care, however, being necessary, as the chromatic scale tolerates much less pedal than the diatonic. (Example 84.)

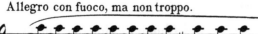

Schubert, Fantaisie, Op.15.

Chromatic scale passages allow, however, the use of the pedal without accompanying notes or chords even for a number of octaves, upon these conditions:

a. If the first and lowest note in a *pp* scale passage is strongly accented, and followed by a crescendo. (Example 85.)

Beethoven, Sonate, Op.27.

Remark. Nicholas Rubinstein was of the opinion that chromatic scale passages could be executed in this manner through the whole compass of the pianoforte, provided the physical strength of the player was sufficient.

Chopin, Scherzo, Op.20.

b. If a strong and constant crescendo is intended in the course of a passage. (Example 86; compare also Examples 38, 40, 41, 54.)

In this latter case the pedal may not only be used where double chromatic notes occur, but even in a succession of chords. (Example 87.)

Balakereff, Islamey.

In the same manner the pedal may be employed in diatonic scale passages for both hands in octaves, thirds, sixths, etc, extending over several octaves. (Examples 88 and 89.)

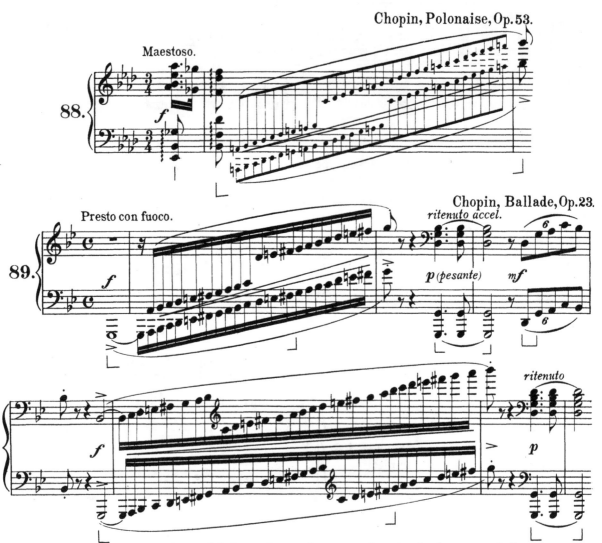

Chopin, Polonaise, Op. 53.

Chopin, Ballade, Op. 23.

In all these latter cases the pedal is employed in proportion to the increase of the crescendo. For this reason a pianist must be possessed of a good amount of physical strength before undertaking a scale passage of several octaves with the pedal, in order to be able to carry out the constantly increasing crescendo.

§ 2. Use of the Pedal in Harmonic Figures.

1. The pedal is pressed down at the beginning of an harmonic figure, and held till a new chord enters, when the process is repeated. (Examples 90 and 91.)

Chopin, Etude, Op. 25.

B. & Co. 2193.

Balakereff, Scherzo.

In cases where the figure begins with the lowest note of a chord, care must be taken that this note is held by the pedal, using afterward the secondary pedal at any harmonic changes where no pause occurs, in order to avoid unclearness. (See Example 90.)

2. An harmonic figure composed of notes in close position admits of less pedal in the lower part of the piano than in the middle and upper part; even in the lower portion the pedal sounds perfectly well if the more open position is employed. (Example 92.)

Liszt, Etude de concert.

The pedal always sounds unclear when used with harmonic figures in close position in the lower portion of the pianoforte, however well the instrument may be in tune. The reason is that the over and under tones assert themselves strongly in this part of the pianoforte.

In the upper portion of the instrument, upon the contrary, a succession of various chords, even, may be played without changing the pedal. (See Example 65.)

34

3. It will readily be seen from the foregoing that, in order to preserve a clear and pure tone in a figure extending from the lower notes over the whole keyboard, the pedal must not be used at the beginning, but somewhat later. (Example 93 a.)

4. Should this figure thereby sound somewhat too dry, the pedal may be employed also at the beginning, but only for a very short time; in the above example, (93 b,) only for a sixteenth (♪).

5. Harmonic figures founded upon the minor chord, and more especially those founded upon the diminished seventh, sound more satisfactorily in the lower part of the instrument than those founded upon the major chord; but even in the first named figures the pedal should only be sparingly used when they occur in that part of the pianoforte.

6. The pedal is most effective in those figures (even in the lower part of the pianoforte) where the passage consists of the overtones of its first (lowest) note. (Examples 94 and 95.)

7. In cases where an harmonic figure (even in close position and in the lower part of the pianoforte) is played simultaneously with a *forte* chord in the middle of the instrument, the pedal may be freely used.

§3. Use of the Pedal in Combined Scale Passages and Harmonic Figures.

1. The pedal sounds well when used with a descending scale passage (especially if played *pp*), following an ascending harmonic figure which serves as a basis for such passage. (Example 96.)

2. Under similar conditions the chromatic scale also sounds clear, (Example 97.)

Chapter VII.
Use of the Pedal with Singles Notes or Chords.

The pedal is often employed with single notes or chords for the purpose of giving additional fulness of tone.

To this intent the pedal may be used.

1. With each separate melodic note, or with every chord which may be long enought to admit of it. (Examples 98 and 99.)

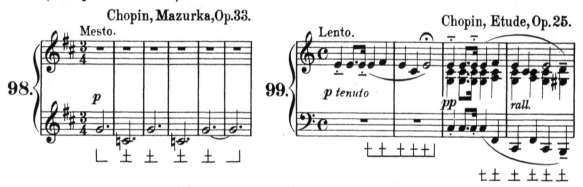

2. In cases where a long note follows, or is followed by, shorter ones, in order to cause a slight crescendo: the pedal should not be used with the shorter notes. (Examples 100—102, see also Example 63.)

3. With single notes or chords, as a means of emphasis. (see example 61.)

4. With very short notes or chords which are followed by long pauses. (Example 103.)

5. Finally, the pedal may be used with repeated notes in order to produce a certain special effect; which seemingly has been used, up to the present time, only by the Rubinstein brothers   This effect is produced by striking repeatedly the same note, making a short, sharp crescendo, whole holding constantly the right pedal, and then, with the addition of the left pedal,* continuing the tone by means of a light pressure; in this way a very long continued and full tone is produced, which dies away very slowly. (Examples 104 and 105.)

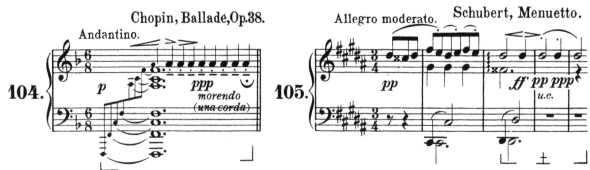

Chapter VIII.

Use of the Ordinary and Tremulo Half Peda .

§1. The ordinary Half Pedal.

1. The ordinary half pedal is used in cases where a long note in the bass cannot be held by the finger, for the reason that the hand is occupied in the upper part of the pianoforte with figures formed of various harmonies, or with a melody having unharmonic notes.   In such cases the down pedal must be employed simultaneously with the *f* bass note, and half raised at any harmonic change, or at the entrance of an unharmonic note in the melody.   While the bass note is not affected, the upper tones receive all the advantages of the pedal. (See Examples 5 and 6.)

Remark. The Schumann composition "For Pedal Piano," played by Anton Rubinstein in his fourth historical concert, furnishes an excellent example of this.

The use of the half pedal is successful in proportion to the depth of the bass note, its distance from the other voices, and the strength with which it is struck.

Remark. The organ fugues of Bach-Liszt contain many examples of the use of the half pedal.

2. In quick and light passages, and also in short snatches of melody, the half pedal can be held uninterruptedly during the whole duration of the long bass note, if the latter is far enough removed from the upper voices, and if no particular clearness and precision of tone are required; but if, con-

* See use of left pedal, Chapter IX, 3.

trary to the highest artistic claims, a certain mist-like, cloudy, or indefinite effect is to be produced. (Example 106, also 6.)

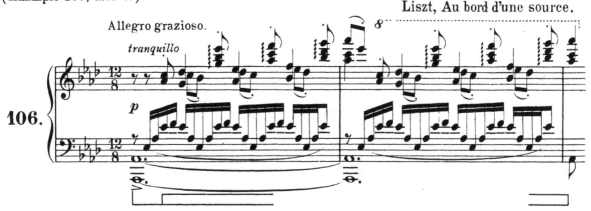

Liszt, Au bord d'une source.

The half pedal can also be successfully used when the upper tones lie nearer the lower long-sustained note; in this case the half pedal must be changed oftener in proportion as the upper tones approach the lower, (*i. e.* by constantly half raising the pedal, which has already been fully pressed down.) The oftener the pedal is raised, the clearer will the bass note stand out.

Remark. The full effect of the half pedal can only be attained upon a good, rich-toned grand piano.

§2. The Tremulo Half Pedal.

When the half pedal is used in such rapid succession that the foot seems almost to vibrate, such use is called, as previously stated, the tremulo half pedal.

Remark. The use of the tremulo, like that of the ordinary half pedal, demands much study. In the former the foot must be pushed a trifle forward, as the tremulo will be found easier of execution in this position. The pedal mechanism must be constructed to yield to a slight foot pressure; a stiff pedal action is inconvenient for this purpose.

The tremulo half pedal is used in cases where the long-vibrating note or chord occurs in the middle of the pianoforte, while the quicker passage begins in the upper, moves through the middle portion, and descends ultimately lower than the note or chord held. The tremulo half pedal makes possible in this way quick passages with the pedal, not only in the upper, but also in the middle parts of the instrument, adding brilliancy and fulness to the tone, and, far from retarding the vibration of the long bass note, adds slightly to its tone. This may be explained by the light, passing contact of the dampers with the thick piano strings.

In the employment of the tremulo half pedal the long note or chord must be played *f*, the passage itself lightly, quickly and *pp*, or at least with a strong diminuendo leading to *pp*. (See Example 7.)

This pedal may also be employed in a quick *pp* passage, even without a long foundation note. (Example 107.)

Chopin, Ballade, Op. 52.

In this example the passage given gains largely in fulness, producing a somewhat mysterious rustling, rushing effect.

It must be remarked that the half raising of the pedal in the middle of the piano is not fully equivalent to the use of the full pedal. In spite of this, however, its use seems thoroughly necessary in modern pianoforte compositions, which often demand three hands, or even more, as without it the exact execution of many such passages would be impossible.

Chapter IX.
The Left Pedal. (Una Corda.)

When the left pedal is pressed down the whole keyboard is moved slightly, so that the hammer touches one string only, thus producing a weaker tone.

Beyond this its employment causes a slight variation in the tone-color, which occurs from the fact that the tone of the string struck is made stronger by the sympathetic vibration of the two untouched strings. The use of this pedal is indicated by the words "una corda," the release of the same by the words "tre corde."

The left pedal is used:

1. To produce the most delicate *pp*, and to give the tone a peculiar coloring. (Examples 108–111.)

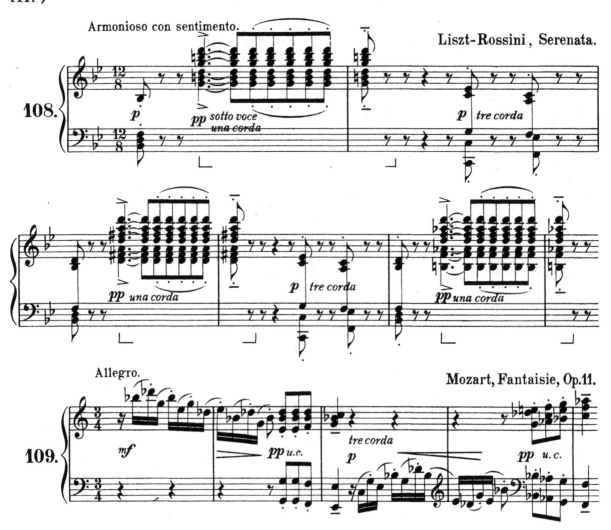

2. To produce the strongest possible contrast between the principal and the accompanying voices, the former being played *f*. (Example 112.)

3. Finally the left pedal may be used for the purpose of softening the concluding notes of a phrase or movement. (Example **113**, also **94**, the last four thirty-seconds $\left(\text{♪}\right)$ in both broken chords; Example **114**, the three last notes of each broken chord.)

Chapter X.

Practical Hints for the Use of the Pedal.

In every case where the pedal is employed the purpose of such use must be taken into consideration. The principal conditions thereto are as follows:

1. The Harmonic Formation of the Piece.

The pedal is generally pressed down simultaneously with the bass note of any given harmony, and raised or changed when any variation therein takes place. (See Chapter IV.)

2. The Melodic Formation.

When two long notes of a melody follow consecutively, the pedal must be changed, even if the notes are harmonically related. This rule must be even more strictly observed when passing or auxiliary notes are used in such passages. (See Chapter IV.)

For exceptions to this rule see Chapter I, Function 15, and Chapter VI.

In cases where the harmony would allow the pedal and a long bass note to be uninterruptedly held, while the melody forbids such method of treatment, either

a. Press the pedal fully down simultaneously with the fundamental bass note, and use the secondary half pedal with every new long melodic note (especially one foreign to the harmony), when the conditions are favorable to such treatment (Chapter VIII); or

b. If the notes foreign to the harmony are short, light, and accompanied by a strong harmonic note upon the accented part of the measure, change the pedal (or release it entirely) simultaneously with the accented note.   (Examples 115 and 116.)

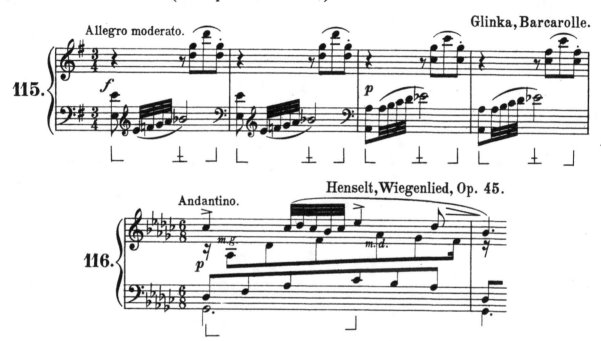

Generally speaking, the shorter the notes foreign to the melody or accompaniment, the lighter they are played, and the more seldom they occur in comparison with the harmonic notes, the more freely may the pedal be uninterruptedly used, so long as the harmony remains the same.   (Examples 117–120; see also Chapter VI, § 1.)

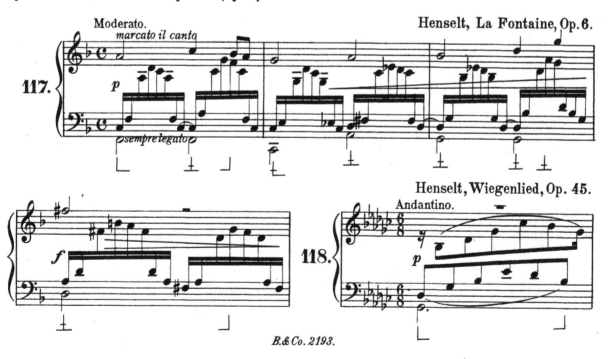

3. Contrapuntal Rules.

The pedal can be held only for a very short time where several melodies or independent voices appear simultaneously; the half pedal may, on the contrary, be held longer.   (Chapter VIII.)

4. Dynamics.

The pedal is used oftener in *f* and crescendo, than in *pp* and diminuendo passages.   If the same phrase is repeated with varying amounts of tone, the pedal is employed oftener in a *f* passage than in the softer one.   (Chapter 1, Functions 11 and 12.)

In a *ff* passage the pedal may even be held uninterruptedly through a whole series of closely following chords.   (Examples 121–123.)

Liszt, Rhapsodie, №6.

Weber, Sonate, Op.39. Menuetto Capriccioso.

5. The Tempo.

A quick tempo allows a more uninterrupted use of the pedal (*i. e.* for a greater number of notes) than a slow tempo, which demands either more frequent changes, or allows generally its use with frequent breaks only.

This difference must be borne in mind even in executing the same phrase in various *tempi*. (Example 124.)

Chopin, Ballade.

6. The Character of the Phrase.

Phrases having an expressive, cantabile, or similar character demand greater use of the pedal than lighter, rapid, and playful ones. (Chapter I, Function 13, and Chapter V, 7.)

44

7. The Character of the Effect Demanded.

When a peculiarly expressive and definite effect is desired in a *pp* passage the use of the right pedal is not recommended, even if permitted by its harmonic structure. (Chapter V, 8.)

When, however, an opposite effect is to be produced, *i. e.* when a mist-like, indefinite effect is indicated by the composer, the pedal may be used freely and at will. (See Chapter I, Function 15, and Examples 125 and 126.)

8. Phrase Divisions.

The pedal must not interfere with a clear separation of phrases, but must serve, on the contrary, to assist this action. (Chapter I, Functions 10, 12, and 13.)

9. Shading.

The pedal serves as an assistance in shading, the down pedal being used with accented notes and crescendo passages, followed by its release when lighter notes or diminuendos take place. (Chapter I, Function 11.)

10. Part of the Piano Used.

The pedal must be more carefully used in the lower than in the middle and upper portions of the pianoforte. (See Chapters V and VI.)

11. The Size of the Hand.

The pianist having a small hand is compelled to resort to a more frequent use of the pedal than one having a larger one. (Chapter I, Functions 2 and 3.)

12. The Properties of the Pianoforte, its Fullness and Purity of Tone.

It will easily be seen from this short review how many conditions must be taken into consideration in order to use the pedal properly.

This little Guide exhausts by no means the various opportunities for its artistic use, as exemplified in the playing of great artists, especially of the Rubinstein brothers. This department forms a rich field for future observation and research. It is to be wished that all persons who interest themselves in music might turn their special attention to the great care taken by great virtuosi in this direction, a study which will be found worthy of their most earnest efforts. The great importance of the pedal to the modern pianist is shown in these words of Anton Rubinstein : " The more I play, the more thoroughly I am convinced that the pedal is the soul of the piano," and " There are cases where the pedal is everything."

B.&Co.2193

BOSWORTH EDITION.

Sir Arthur Sullivan's

Masearade Suite.

**Piano Solo 2/6. Piano duet 5/- (in the press).
Orchestral Score 10/-. Parts 20/-.**

Performed with great success at the Leeds Festival, Manchester, Imperial Institute, Windsor Castle (Her Majesty's Private Band) etc. etc.

The Times says:— The lively strains of the various movements of the masque were greatly enjoyed by the large audience and it is needless to say with what success they were conducted by their composer.—

The Daily Telegraph says:— The Masque from Sir Arthur Sullivan's Merchant of Venice Suite brought all to a brilliant conclusion. These charming and characteristic movements were penned at an hour when Sir Arthur Sullivan's gifts were at their freshest and most buoyant. — There is the exuberance of youth in this dainty and joyous Suite, and the whole, played as it was this morning, made delightful hearing.—

The Yorkshire Post says:— It is bright and sparkling music. In one or two instances the resemblance to favourite tunes in the Savoy operas is delightfully apparent.

The Bradford observer says:— The audience were sent away happy and humming with the echoes of some dainty dances.—

BOSWORTH & Co., LONDON, W.
5, Princes St. Oxford St.

No. 82.   *See over!*

BOSWORTH EDITION.

In Ordering please give Number only. All works are done in excellent cloth binding.

No.	**Piano Studies and Schools.** net	s	d
83.	**Abert, J.** Scales and Chord Studies	1	0
267.	**Beringer, O.** Daily Technical Studies, cplt.	6	0
268.	— — without Scales . . .	5	0
269.	— — Scales and Arpeggios	2	0
270.	— — Modulatory Examples	1	0
109.	**Bertini.** 12 Petits Preludes et Morceaux (H. Germer)	1	0
238.	**Carpé, A.** Grouping, Articulating and Phrasing in Musical Interpretation	6	0
84.	**Clementi, M.** Gradus ad Parnassum (Lebert) . . .	4	0
85.	— 6 Sonatinas (Lebert). Op. 36. . . .	1	4
16.	**Czerny, C.** 100 Studies. Op. 139 (Zwintscher) . .	1	1
17/18.	— The same in 2 Books „ . ea	0	7
19.	— School of Velocity. Op. 299 „ . . .	1	4
20/23.	— The same in 4 Books „ . ea	0	7
24.	— Art of Technic. Op. 740 „ . . .	2	9
25/30.	— The same in 6 Books „ . ea	0	9
34/35.	**Döring, C. H.** Studies. Op. 124. Books 1 and 2 ea	1	8
36/37.	— Op. 125. Books 1 and 2 ea	1	8
10.	**Germer, H.** 20 Melodious Studies	2	0
1/2.	— 100 Elementary Studies. Books 1 and 2 ea	2	3
3/6.	— Practical Teaching Material. 4 Books ea	2	3
7/9.	— School of Sonatina Playing. 3 Books ea	1	6
33.	— Tone Production. New Edition . . .	2	6
78.	— Polyphonic Pianoforte Playing I (Händel, Bach)	1	8
88.	— — — II „	1	8
93, 186/187.	— Etude Primer I, II, III . . . . . . ea	1	6
141.	— Theoretical-Practical School	6	6
142/145.	— Technics. 4 Books (New Edition) . . ea	2	0
131.	— — Complete bound, with 'Tone Production' and 'Musical Ornamentation'	6	6
132.	— Rhythmical Problems	2	6
133.	— Musical Ornamentation. New Edition .	1	3
168/170.	— 36 Pianoforte Studies middle grade, Books 1, 2, 3 ea	2	0
292.	**Haberbier, E.** 12 Poetical Studies (H. Germer) . .	2	0
146/153.	**Heller, St.** Studies. 8 Books (H. Germer) . ea	1	0
96.	**Moore, Gr. P.** First Principles of Technic cplt. { English	3	6
97/98.	— — — I, II ea { Fingering	2	0
218.	— — — cplt. { Foreign	3	6
219/220.	— — — I, II ea { Fingering	2	0
227.	— Lower Division Local school .	1	0
228.	— The Higher Division Local school	1	6
229.	— Candidates Junior Grade Local centre. .	1	6
230.	— Scales Senior Grade Local centre. .	3	0
193.	— "English Scales } separately	2	0
194.	— Fingering" Arpeggi }	1	6
231.	— Supplementary Elementary .	0	9

67 a

BOSWORTH EDITION.

Piano Studies and Schools.

No.				net	s	d
239.	**Moore,Gr.P.**		Lower Division Local school		1	0
240.	—	The	Higher Division Local school		1	6
241.	—	Candidates	Junior Grade Local centre .		1	6
242.	—	Scales	Senior Grade Local centre.		3	0
290.	—	"Foreign	Scales) separately		2	0
291.	—	Fingering"	Arpeggi (		1	6
243.	—		Supplementary Elementary.		0	9
116.	**Petersen, C.**	Children's Piano School .			2	0
32.	—	Elementary Piano School .			2	0
82.	**Piano Pedal Studies** from Rubinstein's Historical Concerts				2	0
293.	**Pischna, J.** Exercises (A. Ruthardt)				2	0
79/81.	**Schmitt, Aloys.** Studies. 3 Books (H. Germer) ea				1	6
31.	**Spindler, F.** Technical Studies				1	6
87.	**Winternitz, R.** Practical Pianoforte School .				3	0

Piano Solos.

			s	d
106.	**Album de Danse III**		1	0
53.	**Album Classique.** Chopin, Field, Mendelssohn, Schubert, Schumann, Weber		1	8
135/136.	**Album of Selected Compositions.** 2 Books (Germer) ea		2	6
176.	**Beethoven, L.** Sonatas complete (Liszt-Edition) . .		5	0
177/178.	— 2 Vols. " ea		3	0
184.	— Sonata Album. 13 Favorite Sonatas .		2	6
109.	**Bertini.** 12 Preludes et Morceaux (H. Germer) . .		1	0
295.	**Borodine, A.** Petite Suite		2	3
42.	**Chopin, F.** Valses (Biehl)		1	0
41.	— Mazurkas "		2	2
38.	— Polonaises "		1	8
39.	— Nocturnes " . . . . . • . .		1	8
40.	— Etudes "		1	8
59.	— Album (Selection). All the popular works. 184 pag. (Biehl)		2	6
72.	— Ballads and Impromptus (Biehl) . . .		1	8
73.	— Scherzos " . . .		1	8
74.	— Rondos and Preludes " . . .		1	8
203/205.	— Favorite Compositions I, II, III (Germer) ea		2	0
224.	**Christmas Album**		1	0
46,50.	**Dance Album I, II** . . . . ea		1	0
15.	**Durra, H.** Shepherd's Idyll		1	8
43.	— Kinderleben (Children's Life)		1	8
171.	**Forino, L.** Album Leaves		2	6
213/214.	**Germer, H.** Echoes of Youth I, II . . . . ea		1	8
44.	— Under the Christmas Tree		1	8
69.	— In the Green Woods		1	8
75/76.	— Joys of Youth I, II. . . . . . ea		1	8
77, 86, 89.	— Elementary Album I, II, III . ea		1	6
47.	**Golden Book of Melody** (R. Kleinmichel)		1	6

				s	d
154.	**Grieg, E.** Op. 3. Poetic Tone Pictures . . .		1	0
155.	— Op. 6. Humoresque		1	0
156.	— Op.17. Norw. Dances and Popular Songs		1	6
157.	— Op.19. Norw. Bridal Procession . .		1	0
158.	— Op.23⁵ from Peer Gynt		1	0
159.	— Op. 12. Eight Lyric Pieces		1	0
245.	— Funeral March		1	0

(braced at right: revised by H. Germer)

				s	d
244.	**Gurlitt, C.** Echoes		1	6
232.	— 6 Bagatelles . . . . . „ . . .		1	6
248.	**Jensen, A.** Wedding Music. 2/ms.		4	0
181.	**Kjerulf, H.** Album Lyrique		2	0
237.	**Kjerulf-Album.** Selection of favorite works (H. Germer)		2	0
210.	**Kuhlau, F.** Rondos (H. Germer)		1	6

67 b

H. GERMER.

BERÜHMTE ALBUMS / CELEBRATED ALBUMS
der BOSWORTH EDITION / of BOSWORTH EDITION

MORCEAUX CÉLÈBRES	MORCEAUX CÉLÈBRES
KJERULF ALBUM	KJERULF ALBUM
_____ ALBUM LYRIQUE	_____ ALBUM LYRIQUE
MENDELSSOHN ALBUM	MENDELSSOHN ALBUM
_____ LIEDER OHNE WORTE	_____ LIEDER OHNE WORTE
SCHUMANN ALBUM .. complet	SCHUMANN ALBUM.... complete
Theil I. II. III.	I. II. III.
_____ JUGEND ALBUM	_____ ALBUM FOR THE YOUNG
TSCHAIKOWSKY ALBUM I. II.	TSCHAIKOWSKY ALBUM I. II.
_____ JUGEND ALBUM	_____ ALBUM FOR THE YOUNG
_____ JAHRESZEITEN	_____ SEASONS

BERÜHMTES UNTERRICHTS MATERIAL. / CELEBRATED TEACHING MATERIAL.

CZERNY-LEMOINE. 100 Etüden	CZERNY-LEMOINE. 100 Etudes
Bd. I. II.	Book I. II.
SCHMITT A. Etüden. Bd. I. II. III.	SCHMITT, A. Etudes. Book I. II. III.
Schule des Sonatinenspieles.	School of Sonatina Playing
Bd. I. II. III.	Book I. II. III.
Praktischer Unterrichtsstoff.	Practical Teaching Material
Bd. I. II. III. IV.	Book I. II. III. IV.

Neue academische Ausgabe No 1-60
einzeln

siehe separates Verzeichnis.

New Academic Classics No 1-60

SERIE A
see separate list, published separately full music size.

No. 258.   Publ. by Bosworth & Co Leipzig.

Albums Célèbres

87

Titles published by Travis & Emery Music Bookshop:

Bathe, William: A Briefe Introduction to the Skill of Song
Bax, Arnold: Symphony #5, Arranged for Piano for Four Hands by Walter Emery
Burney, Charles: An Account of the Musical Performances in Westminster-Abbey
Burney, Charles: The Present State of Music in France and Italy
Burney, Charles: The Present State of Music in Germany, The Netherlands ...
Crimp, Bryan: Solo: The Biography of Solomon
Frescobaldi, Girolamo: D'Arie Musicali per Cantarsi. Primo Libro & Secondo Libro.
Geminiani, Francesco: The Art of Playing the Violin.
Hawkins, John: A General History of the Science and Practice of Music (5 vols.)
Herbert-Caesari, Edgar: The Science and Sensations of Vocal Tone
Herbert-Caesari, Edgar: Vocal Truth
Isaacs, Lewis: Hänsel and Gretel. A Guide to Humperdinck's Opera.
Isaacs, Lewis: Königskinder (Royal Children) A Guide to Humperdinck's Opera.
Lascelles (née Catley), Anne: The Life of Miss Anne Catley.
Mainwaring, John: Memoirs of the Life of the Late George Frederic Handel
Malcolm, Alexander: A Treaty of Music: Speculative, Practical and Historical
Mellers, Wilfrid: Angels of the Night: Popular Female Singers of Our Time
Mellers, Wilfrid: Bach and the Dance of God
Mellers, Wilfrid: Beethoven and the Voice of God
Mellers, Wilfrid: Caliban Reborn - Renewal in Twentieth Century Music
Mellers, Wilfrid: François Couperin and the French Classical Tradition
Mellers, Wilfrid: Harmonious Meeting
Mellers, Wilfrid: Le Jardin Retrouvé, The Music of Frederic Mompou
Mellers, Wilfrid: Music and Society, England and the European Tradition
Mellers, Wilfrid: Music in a New Found Land: ... ... American Music
Mellers, Wilfrid: Romanticism and the Twentieth Century (from 1800)
Mellers, Wilfrid: The Masks of Orpheus: ...... the Story of European Music.
Mellers, Wilfrid: The Sonata Principle (from c. 1750)
Mellers, Wilfrid: Vaughan Williams and the Vision of Albion
Playford, John: An Introduction to the Skill of Musick.
Purcell, Henry et al: Harmonia Sacra ... The First Book, [1726]
Purcell, Henry et al: Harmonia Sacra ... Book II [1726]
Rastall, Richard: The Notation of Western Music.
Rubinstein, Anton : Guide to the proper use of the Pianoforte Pedals.
Simpson, Christopher: A Compendium of Practical Musick in Five Parts
Tans'ur, William: A New Musical Grammar; or The Harmonical Spectator
Tosi, Pier Francesco: Observations on the Florid Song.
Van der Straeten, Edmund: History of the Violoncello, The Viol da Gamba ...
Van der Straeten, Edmund: History of the Violin, Its Ancestors... Vol.1.
Van der Straeten, Edmund: History of the Violin, Its Ancestors... Vol.2.

Travis & Emery Music Bookshop
17 Cecil Court, London, WC2N 4EZ, United Kingdom.
Tel. (+44) 20 7240 2129